But Is It Bullying?

Teaching positive relationships to young children

Margaret Collins

Illustrated by Philippa Drakeford

P·C·P

York St. John College

ISBN: 1 904 315 43 7

Published by Lucky Duck
Paul Chapman Publishing
A SAGE Publications Company
1 Oliver's Yard
55 City Road
London EC1Y 1SP

SAGE Publications, Inc.
2455 Teller Road
Thousand Oaks, California 91320

SAGE Publications India Pvt Ltd
B-42, Panchsheel Enclave
Post Box 4109
New Delhi 110 017

www.luckyduck.co.uk

Commissioning Editors: Barbara Maines and George Robinson
Editorial Team: Mel Maines, Sarah Lynch, Wendy Ogden
Illustrator: Philippa Drakeford
Designer: Sarah Lynch

Printed in the UK by Antony Rowe Limited

© Margaret Collins 2004

Acknowledgements

I am indebted to:

George Robinson and Barbara Maines for permission to include references to their 'No Blame Approach' anti-bullying material

Investors in Health, (the West Sussex Healthy School Programme) for permission to include children's pictures from the 'Challenging Bullying Behaviour' research project

Healthwise for permission to include definitions of what is and what is not bullying.

How to use the CD-ROM

The CD-ROM contains PDF files, labelled 'Worksheets.pdf' which contain worksheets for each lesson in this resource. You will need Acrobat Reader version 3 or higher to view and print these resources.

The documents are set up to print to A4 but you can enlarge them to A3 by increasing the output percentage at the point of printing using the page set-up settings for your printer.

To photocopy the worksheets directly from this book, set your photocopier to enlarge by 125% and align the edge of the page to be copied against the leading edge of the copier glass (usually indicated by an arrow).

A note on gender

Rather than repeat throughout the book the modern but cumbersome 's/he', we have decided to use both genders equally throughout the range of activities. In no way are we suggesting a stereotype for either gender in any activity. We believe that you can adapt if the example you are given does not correspond to the gender of the child in front of you!

A note on the use of terms

The terms 'victim' and 'bully' used here for ease of reference. Use the children's names, not these 'labels' with the children.

Contents

Introduction   6

How to use this book   15

Section 1 – Name-calling   19

    Further activities   25

    Research related activity   28

Section 2 – Teasing   31

    Further activities   38

    Research related activity   42

Section 3 – Physically Hurting People's Bodies   45

    Further activities   52

    Research related activity   55

Section 4 – Verbal Bullying   57

    Further activities   64

    Research related activity   67

Section 5 – Taking, Breaking and Threatening   69

    Further activities   75

    Research related activity   79

Section 6 – Excluding   81

    Further activities   88

    Research related activity   91

Summary   93

    Checklist Part 1   94

    Checklist Part 2   95

    Story picture-books   96

Resources   100

Introduction

This book has been written for teachers of young primary school children as a way of helping the children to understand what bullying is and what bullying isn't. Very young children do not often engage in bullying – but they do frequently behave in a way that is thoughtless, unkind and hurtful. Such hurtful ways of behaving from very young children can be called 'unkind', 'naughty' or 'bad' and need to be curbed. These are often wrongly referred to as bullying. Hurtful behaviour, whether bullying or not, needs to be addressed; it will only cease if everyone concerned knows how to deal with it.

We need to understand what bullying is and what it is not before calling all hurtful behaviour bullying. We should use other names for teasing and unkind behaviour.

Bullying is:

- meant to hurt
- deliberate
- repeated over a period of time.

Bullying manifests itself in several ways, including:

- name-calling
- teasing
- physically hurtful behaviour
- verbally hurtful behaviour
- taking, breaking and threatening behaviour
- excluding.

Why do young children bully?

A young child, small in stature in the world of giant adults, may resort to bullying for several reasons:

- for attention
- to feel power
- to feel in charge
- to feel important.

It is important to meet these needs in positive ways. Children need to feel that they have our attention, that we listen to them and take note of what they say. They need to be given some kind of power and responsibility and to have this recognised. There are times when children should be in charge – of their work and of their play. They begin to feel self-respect if we notice their increasing ability to take responsibility and to make decisions. Children, too, need to feel important – to someone, at some time of the day.

How these early bullying tactics are dealt with could set the pattern for the child's later development. By encouraging children to see the other person's point of view and by helping them to put themselves in the other person's shoes we help children to develop empathy. If children can 'feel' what a bullied person feels they are less likely to bully children themselves.

Changing children's behaviour

If we want to change children's behaviour we have to make them want to change it for themselves. We have to set a pattern that will make them want to conform and behave in a way that elicits praise and a sense of feeling good about themselves.

It is very easy to put all the blame on the bully – to vent our feelings or distaste about their behaviour – not so easy to ignore it and to concentrate on the person who is being bullied. I suggest that while employing the No Blame Support Group Approach (Robinson and Maines, 2000) with young children we can also work towards improving the behaviour of all the children in the group.

Be positive

It is nearly always possible to find something good to say about or to a child. One method is to try to make ten positive remarks to each child for each negative one. This is not easy to achieve, but in trying to do this we will be on the right lines. For example, if a child is always teasing or spoiling someone's work to get attention – ignore that and try to find positive things to say about her attitude, progress, work or helpfulness in some other capacity. The old saying 'she's only doing it for attention', while being true, means that the child needs attention and we should try to give it in some positive way rather than identifying misdemeanours.

Prompt rather than nag

It's all too easy to say, "You're still doing…", "You're doing…again", "Don't…" Try to remind young children in a positive way not to do some of the things that are anti-social or could be thought of as bullying. Better to say, "Let's remember to do…" or "Can we all remember to…" (for example, "…be kind, be thoughtful to everyone else, put our work here or walk in the corridor, today.")

Descriptive praise

Don't only use exclamations such as 'brilliant', 'super' or 'great'. These can make some, but not all, children feel happy and successful. Try a calmer kind of praise that involves noticing all the little things that a child is doing right even when behaving badly. Motivate children to want to please you – praise is the key to motivation as children want nothing more than approval. Descriptive praise requires us to know exactly what we want the children to do; watch them carefully and notice every step in the right direction, (even better if you remember to say their name first!).

Instead of, "That's a nice picture," say, "Mary, I like the way you've used those colours." Instead of "well done" when a child allows someone into the line say, "James, that is kind of you to let Harry in." This kind of descriptive praise not only makes James feel good about his behaviour, it also promotes your message to everyone and highlights the kinds of behaviours that please you.

Reflective listening

Reflective listening is imagining what children might be feeling and helping them to put it into words.

Help them to get their feelings out into the open; by naming feelings they can come to terms with them. Show that you understand how they feel and say that it is OK to feel like that, but help them to understand that anti-social behaviour cannot be excused if they allow themselves to give way to their feelings. For example, if a child is angry at not being allowed to use the computer or because someone else is chosen to do a task, saying something such as "it must be really hard for you to work on paper when you really want to use the computer" will help. Allow them to express the feelings and discuss them rather than feeling impotence and rage against the one who was chosen.

Helping children to get their feelings out into the open and treating their feelings with respect is a good way of preventing children from retaliating angrily against the other person involved.

Talk about feelings

Children can often feel frustrated, angry, left out, hard done by and neglected. By talking about these kinds of feelings – perhaps in Circle Time – we help children to realise that we all feel like that at times. Treat their feelings with respect and talk about how to deal with them.

Explain that it's OK to say:

- ▸ "I don't like it when you do that," but less acceptable to say, "I don't like you when you do that."
- ▸ "It makes me feel sad when you..." rather than, "You're horrid when..."

Setting rules

Children like rules, especially if you have given them a hand in setting them out. Involve children in setting rules and behaviours stated as positives rather than negatives. Children like to know what framework of behaviour is acceptable to you. They feel safe in knowing that others must keep to the rules. Your part is in making sure that all children keep to the rules.

Consistent treatment throughout the school

It's not only in the classroom that children need consistent handling – behaviour in the playground, dinner hall, corridors, library, lavatories needs consistency by those in charge. All adults are role models and children learn from the behaviour of adults around them. Do the classroom assistants, mid-day supervisors, cleaners, parent helpers behave in the same consistent way with children? Do they behave towards each other with the same consideration? Children learn from what they see and if they see anger, petty mindedness or other undesirable personal qualities displayed in the school they will see this as acceptable behaviour.

'Challenging Bullying Behaviour'

This is the title of a report of a research project carried out in West Sussex. The research team worked with 439 children and their teachers from eight primary schools. (Tomkins, Wetton and Collins, 2003) Some of the activities in this book use the youngest children's comments and pictures they drew and are reproduced here with kind permission of Investors in Health (the West Sussex Healthy School Programme).

The youngest children saw bullying as mainly physical, while Year 2 showed a growing awareness of verbal bullying.

When asked what kind of behaviour they thought was bullying:

- ▸ Year R gave 7 categories of behaviour, e.g. hitting, punching.
- ▸ Year 1 gave 50 categories, such as hurting, laughing at, poking, hitting with sticks.
- ▸ Year 2 gave 61 categories, e.g. kicking, pulling hair, calling names, spitting.

When asked about the feelings of a bullied child:

- Year R only used the two words, 'sad' and 'unhappy'.
- Year 1 children used ten different words, such as 'grumpy', 'scared', 'upset'.
- Year 2 children used 17 different words, e.g. 'lonely', 'mournful', 'worried'.

If we are to help children to understand more about what bullying is and the feelings of a bullied person it is crucial to spend time talking about feelings and helping young children to develop a 'language or vocabulary of feelings'.

Bullying Survey

At the end of the book is a two page bullying survey. You may like to use this (or your own amended version) with your children before you start working through the activities to determine their feelings about what bullying is and what it is not. Take note of the total class responses and then repeat the survey after you have done the activities you have chosen to work through. In this way you will be able to evaluate, measure and discuss the children's changed perceptions of bullying.

You could:

- read it out in Circle Time to young children– omitting parts that are not appropriate and counting their responses
- ask older children to complete it and not put names on their paper to provide you with a discussion document.

Hopefully, if you work through the activities in this book, they should get it right!

No Blame Support Group Approach (Robinson and Maines 2000)

This seems to me to be the most effective approach when dealing with bullying in school.

You will need to:

- provide a secure warm environment for your discussion and enlist the help of the supporting group
- make sure that you don't apportion blame to the bully in your discussion
- make sure that nobody thinks that being a bully works by giving the attention they seek for their negative actions
- make sure you use every opportunity to praise everyone involved when positive circumstances occur.

The seven steps of the No Blame Approach to Bullying

Aims:

- to keep the 'victim' safe
- to obtain empathetic support from the participants including the bully
- to empower onlookers/colluders.

Step 1 – talk with the victim

Initiate a warm conversation with the bullied child, asking her or him to tell you about what happened and how it made them feel. Discuss who is involved in the hurtful behaviour. Note whether this is a single incident or part of persistent behaviour from one or a group of children. Ask the child to draw or write down how they felt.

Step 2 – convene a meeting with children involved

Gather a group of children who have been involved – bully(ies), bystanders and observers – six to eight is a good number. Balance the group with friends and supporters of the victim. The composition of a healthy group is essential and the group does not include the victim.

Step 3 – explain the problem to the group

In a warm conversation explain your own worries about the victim's feelings – read out what the bullied person wrote or show their picture – don't discuss the actual bullying event. Be only concerned with how the bullied person sees the hurtful behaviour and how it makes them feel.

Resist listening to excuses from the group and don't allocate any blame to anyone.

Step 4 – share responsibility

It is very important to explain that nobody is in trouble, to be blamed nor punished.

The group's task is to take on the responsibility of trying to make the victim happy and secure. Explain that their task is to do this individually and in their own way.

Step 5 – ask the group members for their ideas

Encourage each member to suggest what they can do to make the victim happier.

Make sure they use 'I' language of intention, for example, 'I will...', 'I can...'

You can make a note of what each member suggests they do, but ownership of these supportive ideas must come from the children themselves and not be imposed by you. If you do make a note of a child's intention, give it to that child as a validation, don't keep it as a record.

Step 6 – leave it up to them

Remind them that you are handing over the responsibility to the group.

Explain that you will meet members of the group, individually, in about a week to see how things are going.

Step 7 – meet them again

About a week later meet each child individually (including the 'victim') to see how things are going. Reassure them all that you will monitor the 'victim' who can come to talk to you if they have any problems.

More details of this approach are available at www.luckyduck.co.uk.

To be effective this approach has to be a whole-school initiative.

Everyone on the staff has to agree to this approach – this includes classroom helpers, mid-day meal supervisors, kitchen staff and the caretaker. Include this approach in your behaviour policy and as part of your home/school agreement, making sure that parents know why you use it.

A parents' and carers' meeting would be a useful way of including them in the approach, with regular updates for new parents or carers.

In *Bullying Matters*, Noreen Wetton and Margaret Collins devised the following definitions of bullying.

"We think that Key Stage 1 children will be able to understand this definition:

It is bullying when people:

▸ hurt others on purpose –with words or by hitting or kicking
▸ say they will hurt them
▸ tease others unkindly
▸ call people names
▸ take their things, spoil or throw them away
▸ say unkind things about others, whether true or not
▸ prevent others from joining in their work, play or group activities.

It is not bullying when people:

▸ hurt you by accident
▸ don't know you want to join in
▸ won't let you have your own way
▸ ask you to wait your turn
▸ want you to go by the rules
▸ borrow or use your things and forget to ask you, especially if they do not realise the things are not for general use.

We think that Key Stage 2 children will be able to understand this definition:

It is bullying when people:

▸ deliberately hurt others, time after time, especially when they are unable to defend themselves
▸ tease others, especially when the person getting teased begins to feel unhappy about it
▸ call others names, for example referring to race, colour, culture, gender or any form of disability in a negative way
▸ threaten that they will hurt others
▸ try to take possessions or money by force
▸ demand that others give money or possessions
▸ force others to do things they know they should not do
▸ hurt others physically
▸ spoil, damage, take or throw away other people's belongings
▸ leave people out of play, groups or other social activities deliberately and frequently

- exaggerate tales or spread rumours particularly when meaning harm to the person
- act maliciously towards others, openly or by stealth
- make offensive remarks, hiss or otherwise show that they are intending to hurt or dominate others.

It is not bullying when people:

- borrow things and forget to return them
- ask if they can join in
- call you by a name you are happy with
- hurt you accidentally
- explain why you cannot be included in a group activity."

How to use this book

Bullying can take several forms and can be expressed in words, behaviour and in more subtle ways such as social group process, body language and facial expressions. This book has taken six areas of behaviour as headings for each section; inevitably there is some overlap as some kinds of behaviour fall into several categories.

The sections are:

- ▶ name-calling
- ▶ teasing
- ▶ physical bullying
- ▶ verbal bullying
- ▶ taking, breaking and threatening
- ▶ excluding.

You will find activities for children in these six sections to promote awareness of what bullying is and what it isn't.

You can work through the book from start to finish or dip into it to select activities to help children to cope with particular incidents in school.

Format

Each section has the following format:

- ▶ Poster – each section starts with a poster as a trigger for discussion about children's behaviour. Be very aware of the children in your class and sensitive to any issues that might be very personal to them.

- ▶ Poster related activities – in which children are directed to explore the feelings of the people depicted and discuss what they say, relating it to their own feelings if they were in the same position.

- ▶ Further activities – more ways to explore the theme.

- ▶ Research related activity.

- ▶ Review – where children are reminded of the main points of the theme.

In each section there are suggestions for the kinds of books to use. Ideas for displaying the children's work form an integral part of each section.

By using these activities and through discussion you can help children to realise they have a positive role to play in:

- being thoughtful about other people's feelings
- being careful about other people's bodies
- not bullying other children
- not encouraging other children to bully
- acting as a concerned bystander if they see unkind, hurtful behaviour (or bullying) taking place and getting help or doing something about it.

Remind all children – frequently:

There is only one thing for a child to do if she is being bullied and that is to get help from a responsible and safe adult.

There is only one thing for a child to do if he sees someone bullying and that is to get help from a responsible and safe adult.

The CD

The CD contains the posters in full colour as well as the individual drawings as larger single pictures.

You can print off on A3 using your school printer or take the CD to a print shop and ask them to print off the full colour posters in any size you wish, but check the prices first as this can be expensive.

The CD also contains the bullying checklists from pages 94 and 95. You can print these for the children to use or amend them as appropriate to your own requirements.

How to use the posters

There are several pages of suggestions about how to use the posters for discussion followed by other 'further activities' for the children.

You can use the poster discussions as your input time in Circle Time and several of the further activities also lend themselves to Circle Time work.

Initially, display the poster on one of your wallboards, in glorious isolation with plenty of space around it.

As the children complete work about that aspect of bullying, display their pictures and writing around the poster.

Ask the children to suggest appropriate speech bubbles asking questions and giving suggestions about the work and about bullying.

Use quotes from the children's work to make this a lively and interactive display.

Use the display by occasionally reading the speech bubbles with the children.

Draw attention to the display if there are any incidents of unkind or hurtful behaviour (or bullying) and remind the children of what they have drawn and said about that kind of behaviour.

Section 1 – Name-calling

Children call people names
for many reasons.
Often it is just for fun,
or because they don't know
the person's real
name. In this section we
explore the many reasons
for name calling
and look out for occasions
when it is, or can turn
into, bullying.

Name-calling?

Section 1 – Name-calling

Show the poster to the children and first talk about what the children are doing. Explain that it is a school playground with children playing in the dinner playtime. You might find it more profitable to do a few of the speech bubble activities each day rather than to try to do all these at the same time. Display the poster on the wall.

Add children's work as you complete the activities.

Poster related activities

'Throw it to me, Stupid'

Look at the speech bubble and read it out to the children. Ask the children to raise a hand if someone has ever called them 'Stupid' and count how many hands are raised. Ask volunteers to tell you how that made them feel.

> Calling someone stupid makes them feel...
>
> | unhappy | hurt |
> |---------|------|
> | worried | small |
> | sad | |
>
> bad inside
> they can't do things
> they'll keep getting it wrong
> always useless

▸ Did any of them feel happy about this?
▸ Did any of them feel hurt?
▸ Did it help them to do whatever they were doing better?
▸ Did it make things worse?

Read through your list with the children and ask them to show by their faces and body language how they would feel if someone called them 'Stupid'. Ask children what they would say to a child who called someone else 'Stupid'.

'You're first again, Speedy'

Look at this speech bubble. Ask the children how they think this child feels, when someone calls her 'Speedy'. Collect up the feelings words and make a list. Put this list alongside the list from the previous activity and look at the words the children gave you.

Ask the children to stand up and work in pairs with one saying, "You're first again, Speedy," and to show by their faces and by their body language how they would feel.

> If someone called me 'Speedy' I'd feel...
>
> great
> fast
> super
> a good runner
> a sportsman
> a good player
> good inside.

'Hurry up, Slowcoach'

Ask the children to tell you what they think is happening here – is it a mother taking her child to school or could it be something else?

Why do they think the child is lagging behind? Collect up the children's responses and talk about them.

How do they think the child feels when the mother calls him 'Slowcoach'? Do you think this will make the child hurry up?

What else could the mother say to the child that would make him hurry?

Slowcoach

I think the boy would feel...

sad
unhappy
slow
unwilling
worried.

I think the boy could feel good if it's a fun name in the family.

Ginger

She has ginger hair.
She likes to eat ginger biscuits.
It means she is quick.
It's like her name 'Jean Jones'.
Her family call her Ginger.
She likes her friends to call her Ginger.
19 of us think she likes it. 7 of us think she doesn't like it.

'Ginger's on my side'

Ask the children to tell you why they think someone might call a girl 'Ginger' and collect their responses.

Ask them to think if this could be a good or unkind name to call someone.

Ask them to put a thumb up if they think it is a good name and down if it is a bad name. Count the thumbs.

Ask volunteers to say why.

'Come and play with us, Lofty'

Look at the picture of Lofty and the smaller children who want him to play with them.

Does Lofty look happy? Do you think it's an unkind name or a fun name? Do you think he likes being called that name? Why?

How do you think Lofty feels when people use the name Lofty? Draw a picture of Lofty feeling part of the crowd when people use that name.

Lofty

Lofty feels proud when people call him that. He likes being tall.

'Get up, Crybaby'

Can you think of a time when someone called you a Crybaby? Put your thumb down if someone has called you a Crybaby. How did you feel?

Collect and list the words the children give you. Do you think it helped the little girl to be called Crybaby? What would you say to the children who called her a Crybaby? What would you say to the person who is crying? What could you do to help?

'You're my best friend, Frizzy Lizzie'

Look at the picture of Frizzy Lizzie. Her real name is Elizabeth, but her family call her Liz. She likes that. Why do you think her friend calls her Frizzy Lizzie?

Does she look happy about it? Do you think it is good to call her that? Why? Would you like to be called Frizzy Lizzie if you looked like her?

Frizzy Lizzie
We all think she would like to be called that because her best friend wouldn't say it if she knew she didn't like it.

THAT'S ME!

'You're a real wally'

Talk to the children about using names such as 'wally' when talking to other children. Do they know the Wally books which show Wally as a fun figure engaged in lots of interesting activities? Or do they see 'wally' as a name to use to someone who is not very clever or good at things?

Explain that Walter is a real name that is sometimes shortened to Wally. It is sometimes used as a fun or loving way to talk to people. It is also used as a horrid name about people, meaning that they are not very clever.

Explain that it is not only the name that we use that is important but the way our voice sounds when we use it. Have they seen the TV advertisement for Yellow Pages, where the actor has badly cut the child's hair and takes her to the hairdresser to get it cut well? The actor talks to the hairdresser in a very aggressive way, but the words he uses are very kind words.

YOU'RE A REAL WALLY!

Explore with the children different ways of saying 'You're a real wally'. Ask them to work in pairs and say it:

▸ in a loving way   ▸ in an angry way
▸ in a sad way   ▸ in a happy way
▸ in an excited way.

Further activities

But is it bullying?
Explain to the children that calling people names can be a kind of bullying.

It all depends on the names they use. Using unkind names that are about someone's family, their colour or religion is always bullying, especially if it is done to hurt someone, is done on purpose and is done over and over again.

Explore with the children how they would feel if someone called them a really horrid bullying name. Refer to any recent relevant incidences and talk about the feelings of all the people involved.

Remind the children that it is important to use only names that other people are happy about and to think about how the other person feels. Ask them to think about these five points.

1. Will she like me using this name?
2. If I use this name will it hurt their feelings or will it be fun for everyone?
3. Could he feel bad or upset if I use this word about what he is doing?
4. Is my voice using the name in a way that could make them happy or upset?
5. If I use this name could it make them angry and want to hurt me back?

Other names
Talk about the names that the children in the poster used. Some are complimentary names and children will like to be called that. Ask volunteers to give you names that they would like people to call them. Others were not so complimentary and children could be hurt. Talk to the children about other names that could really hurt people. Can they tell you some? How do the children feel about people using these names?

Fun names
In Circle Time ask the children to think about their name and ask each child to stand up, say their name and sit down again.

Talk with the children about other names – names that people like to have, but that are not really their names.

Sometimes these names are:

▸ about the job the person has – the crossing patrol, the fireman
▸ shortened names that people like to use, for example, Steve for Steven, Bill for William

- fun names that describe people, such as, 'Curly' or 'Blondie' describe hair; 'Samson' describes a strong person
- funny, such as 'Little John' who was a giant of a man in the Robin Hood stories.

Ask the children if they can give you some odd or fun names they know from stories or TV.

Talk about how people feel if others use these 'nicknames'. Most people like it – it shows they are friendly, but sometimes people don't like it, especially if the names are meant to be hurtful. Explain to the children that they should only use other names if they are really sure that the person likes to be called by that name.

Nicknames I know
Ask the children to think of good nicknames that they know about people in books, on TV, in their own family or people they know. Ask volunteers to finish the sentence: 'I know someone whose nickname is…because…'

Ask the children to close their eyes and think about themselves, their name and how they look. Can they think of a nickname that they would like people to use for them? Go around the circle asking the children to complete this sentence: 'My real name is…but friends can call me…'

Hurtful names
Ask the children to close their eyes and think of a time when someone has used a hurtful name about them and how they felt. Give examples of some of the hurtful names, such as 'silly' or 'slow' and ask the children to help you to make a list. Then ask the children to tell you how they think people feel when others use unkind or hurtful names about them.

> ## Hurtful names
>
> It's hurtful when someone calls people:
>
> | | |
> |---|---|
> | silly | stupid |
> | daft | careless |
> | slow | dirty |
> | a baby | crybaby |
> | thick | brainless |

> ## Feelings words
>
> You feel...
>
> | | |
> |---|---|
> | unhappy | sad |
> | worried | low |
> | nervous | upset |
> | hurt | wounded |

Collect these responses and make a list. Talk with the children about how these feelings can sometimes make things worse. Ask them to make sure that they think carefully before using names that will hurt other people. Tell them that they should only use fun or nicknames if they are certain that the people like to be called by those names.

Pat's the name

Tell the children the story of a girl called Gertrude who doesn't like her name. Her family call her Pat, but at school the teachers use her real name because it is on the school register and on her birth certificate.

Ask the children to tell you why they think she doesn't like her name. Collect their responses. What do you think the teacher should do? What do you think the children should do? Ask the children how they would feel if they didn't like their own name. What could they do?

I'M PAT!

Pat's the name

Gertrude is old fashioned.
It doesn't sound nice.
It sounds 'rude'.
She is used to being called Pat.
No-one else is called Gertrude.

Helping Yavu

We could...
help him with his work
show him how to keep it tidy
be a good friend to him
tell him he is useful
make a joke about things
help him to feel better
say that it doesn't matter.

We could say, "Cheer up Yavu, we all make mistakes, I'll help you to put it right."

You're useless

Yavu was six years old and he was a bit clumsy. His parents worried about him. He used to break things or put things down in a messy or untidy way. His teachers worried about him – his writing was untidy and his work was messy. Some people said he was useless.

Yavu began to think he really was useless and things got worse. He became very unhappy and stopped trying to do better. In the playground he dropped the ball and was no good at games. If he ran he bumped into people and sometimes hurt them. If Yavu was in your class, what could you do to help him?
What could you say to help Yavu?

Pet names

Ask the children to think of some of the names that people use about people that they love. Ask volunteers to help you to make a list.

Can they tell you who uses these names and who they use them about? Ask volunteers to finish this sentence: 'Mum or Dad calls me…when she or he is pleased with me.' Ask them how they feel when parents/carers use these special names. Do the children know any special names that people use about their pets?

Sometimes pure bred animals have long registered names and people choose a short pet name to use. Ask the children to try to find out some of these by asking their families or looking at books.

Research related activity

What should a person do if people call them names?

In the bullying research mentioned on page 9 a Year 1 child drew this picture and wrote about what she thought she could do if she was bullied or saw someone being bullied. Tell your children that a Year 1 child said this and ask them to think about whether this is the best thing to do.

What should you do if someone calls you names?

13 said tell the teacher.
9 said don't tell.
3 said tell your friend.
2 said don't do anything.

Ask children to raise one thumb if they think this is the best thing to do and count their responses. Ask volunteers to tell you why they think this is the best thing to do.

Ask children to put one thumb down if they think this is not the best thing to do. Count their responses and ask volunteers to say why.

Ask the children to think of other things a child could do and jot these down.

Talk with all the children about the best thing to do in your school if someone calls them names.

- ▸ Talk about names that are hurtful.
- ▸ Talk about names that are not meant to hurt.
- ▸ Talk about people who might keep on calling them names.

Repeat the activity, but this time about someone (a bystander) who sees someone else calling a child names.

> **What should you do if you see someone calling someone names?**
>
> 3 said tell the teacher.
> 5 said don't tell.
> 4 said tell your friend.
> 2 said don't do anything.
> 10 said 'go and comfort the person'.

Are your children's responses the same for both occasions?

Make two charts of all their responses and add these charts to the display. During your work on this theme, use your library to look out for – and encourage children to find – story picture-books with characters with unusual (or hurtful) names, even though these may not be about bullying.

Books such as:

▶ Fitzpatrick, M. (1999) *Izzy and Skunk*, David & Charles Children's books

▶ Hughes, S. (1993) *Dogger*, Red Fox

▶ King-Smith, D. (1996) *Omnibombulator*, Young Corgi

▶ Hoffman, M. (1987) *Nancy No Size*, Mammoth Books

▶ Browne, A. (1995) *Willy the Wimp*, Walker Books

▶ Richardson, J. (2002) *Grunt*, Random House.

You may also like to use *Why Charlie Brown, Why?*, by C. M. Schulz which tells the story of Janice who has leukaemia. She loses her hair and is called Baldy by a schoolmate until everyone realises that she is ill.

Review

After you have finished this section about name-calling talk with the children about their work and what they have achieved. Look again at the poster and at the display you have made. Ask the children to tell you which of the name-calling activities of the children in the poster are most likely to be called bullying. Are there any at all?

Ask the children to help you to agree a final speech bubble to add to the display, which will tell other people what they think about name-calling. Share, with other classes or with parents and carers, this poster and the work you have done. Make sure that everyone in your school knows what they should do if:

▶ somebody bullies by calling someone names
▶ they see or hear someone bullying by name-calling.

Session 2 – Teasing

Children like to tease each other and usually this is good fun. Occasionally it can get out of hand and turn into a kind of bullying behaviour. In this section we explore the different kinds of teasing and identify occasions when it could be bullying.

Section 2 – Teasing

Talk with the children about teasing and what it really is. Have they ever seen someone tease a pet? Do they think this is kind? Is teasing really fun and playing or can it be unkind and horrid?

Explain that teasing is only good when the person being teased is enjoying it. Talk about the scenarios on the poster with the children, reading out each section and discussing it as below.

Display the poster on the wall. Add children's work as you go through the activities.

Poster related activities

I'm not teasing it
Ask the children to think about Jin-ho and the kitten.

Ask, "Is he playing with the kitten or teasing it?" and collect their responses. Talk about when fun teasing turns into hurtful or horrid teasing. How do they think Jin-ho is feeling?

> **Jin-ho feels...**
>
> | | |
> |---|---|
> | happy | big |
> | funny | clever |
> | playful | powerful |
> | glad | important |

Collect these responses and make two lists – good feelings about playing with the kitten and not so good feelings about teasing.

Talk about how people feel when they are teasing someone and that sometimes these not so good feelings get worse and turn into bullying.

Ask the children to walk around the room – or inside the circle – showing with their face and body each of these good feelings in turn.

Ask the children what the kitten could do to Jin-ho.

He's got my cap
Billy and Juan are really good friends but on this day Billy snatched Juan's cap and started to run away with it.

> **Juan's cap**
>
> 8 think it is a good game.
> 18 think it is not. Billy could use a ball or something else to play with.

Ask the children to tell you how they think Billy feels. Ask them how they think Juan feels.

Count up how many think this is a good game and how many think this is unkind. Explain that a game or 'playing' is only good fun if everyone feels happy about it.

She's pulling my scarf

Ask volunteers to say what is happening here.

Do they think that the girl with the scarf is happy about this?

Ask them to think about what could happen – to the girl, to the teaser and to the scarf. Do they think that someone could get hurt?

Ask the children to go and draw their own quick picture about what happens next.

Come together into a group, collect the pictures and share them with the group.

I think...

The scarf could come away from the girl's neck and the one pulling it could fall over.

Count up how many children's pictures show that this is fun and how many show that it is unkind.

Explain to the children that this is a kind of bullying – especially if it happens again and again and the person pulling the scarf really means to hurt or the child with the scarf is unhappy.

Who is it?

Asif is seven and thinks he is playing. He comes up behind Sarah, who is five, and covers her eyes with his hands and says, "Who is it?"

This frightens Sarah and makes her start to cry.

Ask the children to close their eyes and to think how this makes Sarah feel. Ask volunteers to tell you.

Ask the children:

▶ 'What would you say to Asif?'
▶ 'What would you say to Sarah?'
▶ 'Do you think this is bullying?'

SORRY SARAH

None of us thinks this is bullying, but we think Asif was not thinking ahead when he did it.
He should say he is sorry and comfort Sarah.

Ask the children to think of what happens next.
Ask them to draw this picture – about what Asif and Sarah do next. Ask them to write a caption for their picture telling what happened next.

It's only a game

Benazir is complaining to the teacher that someone has taken her book and two girls are playing with it. Ask the children to think if this is bullying.

Ask them to raise one hand if they think it is and ask volunteers to say why.

Ask them to raise a fist if they think it is not bullying and ask volunteers to say why.

Ask the children what they think the teacher should do and make a list of their suggestions.

Ask the children how they think Benazir is feeling.

Ask volunteers to say what they could do to help Benazir.

Make a list of these responses to display near the poster.

The teacher could...

▸ tell Benazir to go and ask for it back
▸ go and talk to the two girls
▸ say the girls are only playing
▸ make the girls give it back and play somewhere else.

I haven't got it!

Someone has taken Harry's bag and thrown it to someone else. Ask the children if this kind of thing has ever happened to them – someone taking something of theirs and pretending they haven't got it.

If so, ask volunteers to tell you what happened to them Ask the children to think whether this kind of teasing is really bullying.

Ask volunteers to tell you how they think Harry is feeling and make a list of these feelings words.

Talk about these feelings and help the children to add to them.

We think Harry feels...

▸ sad
▸ upset
▸ angry
▸ fed up
▸ cross
▸ unhappy
▸ alone.

Ask the children to choose one of these feelings for Harry. Choose places for the children to stand and show the feeling they chose, for example, stand by the door if you think Harry feels sad or stand by the window if you think Harry feels cross.

Ask them to show by their face how this feels and share these faces with other groups.

Can't you take a joke?

Ash has taken Shiraz's ball and he is very upset. Ask the children if they think this is a good joke and count up the numbers who say 'yes' and 'no'.

I don't think it is a joke because Ash is bigger than Shiraz. The teacher is coming to help.

Ask the children to close their eyes and to think what might happen next.
Ask them to open their eyes and go and draw a picture of what happened.
Show and talk about their pictures; discuss their ideas for a good solution.

Boo!

Amelia is always creeping up on children in the playground and making them jump. Sometimes she shouts, "Boo!" sometimes she claps her hands or makes a loud noise. She thinks it's funny. Shona hates being startled like this. Ask the children to close their eyes and think whether Amelia is teasing or whether this is a kind of bullying. Ask the children to go and stand in a particular place if they think it is bullying. Count how many children think this is bullying and note whether girls are more likely to say it is bullying than boys.

Ask the children to tell you what Shona could do and make a list of what the children say. What do they think they themselves could say to Amelia?

Look again

Ask the children to look again at the eight pictures on the poster. Ask them to look at these pictures to decide which (if any) of these teasing pictures they think could really be bullying. Number the pictures and ask the children to think about which are:

- ▶ fun or happy teasing
- ▶ not so good teasing that could turn into bullying
- ▶ bullying.

Ask younger children to tell you what they think and make a note of what they say. Make a chart to show what they think – use the three headings and ask children to draw pictures of the children to add to the chart. Display this alongside the poster.

Ask older children to work in pairs or threes and make a list of what they think before coming together into a group to talk about and justify their decisions. Ask them to make a tidy copy of their list and to illustrate it. Add this work to the display alongside the poster.

Further activities

Tickling

Ask the children to raise a hand if they are ticklish. Ask volunteers to tell you how they feel about people tickling them. Ask the whole group to raise a thumb if they don't mind being tickled and to turn their thumb down if they don't like being tickled.

Ask the children if they think that tickling can be a kind of bullying. Remind the children that bullying can be when someone does something hurtful or horrid on purpose and does this again and again, meaning to hurt you.

Ask the children to go and stand in one of three places:

Tickling

8 of us like being tickled.
7 of us don't like being tickled.
6 of us like being tickled sometimes.

‣ Place one is where children who like being tickled go.
‣ Place two is where children who don't like being tickled go.
‣ Place three is where children who like it sometimes and don't like it sometimes go.

Ask the children to count themselves by standing in a line then one person at the end of the line starts by saying 'one', the rest say 'two', 'three' and so on. Count up and make a chart of their numbers. Ask children to draw themselves being tickled and show how they feel. Help children to write labels or titles and add the chart and some pictures to your display.

Ask older children to write about a time when someone tickled them and to say how this made them feel. Share these pictures with the whole group and put them into three groups as above. Ask children within each group to vote on one picture from their group to add to the display.

Who's different today?

Remind the children that we are all the same in many ways and yet we are all different and special. Ask them to raise a thumb if they have, for example:

‣ brown eyes
‣ black hair
‣ long hair
‣ long nails.

Ask volunteers to tell you how they are special or different.

Tell the children this story about Huma.

> Huma was new to the school and didn't have many friends. She had to wear glasses because she could not see very well. One day Huma broke her glasses and could not do her work very well. In the playground a group of children started teasing Huma because she looked different without her glasses and because her work was not good.

Ask volunteers to tell you how they thought Huma was feeling when people teased her. Ask volunteers to tell you how they thought the teasers felt.

Poor Huma

I would tell Huma to take no notice and to come and play with me.
I might tell the playground teacher.

Ask the children whether they think this was bullying or not and count up the numbers of 'yes' and 'no'.

Ask the children to draw a picture and write about what they could do to make Huma feel better.

Jarra's no good at football

Tell the children this story about Jarra.

> Jarra was always missing the ball when they played football. One day children started teasing and taunting him by shouting in the playground, "Jarra's no good at football." This made Jarra start to cry and the children teased him more. Jarra's big brother came to help, but the children said they were only teasing him.

Ask the children to think about what Jarra's brother could say and do. Ask volunteers to tell you. Make a note of what they say and afterwards ask children to choose the best thing to say and do.

He's had his hair cut

Jonny wanted to have his hair cut in one of the new fashionable ways, with bits shaved off in a pattern, to be like other boys in his class. His mum didn't want to do this but he persuaded her to let him have it done. He felt really cool when he got to school the next day. Most of the boys liked his haircut, but some of the girls started to 'take the mickey'. They teased him about his hair and made up silly rhymes about him.

Jonny was very upset and when he got home he told his mum and sister, but that didn't help him to feel any better.

Do the children think this is teasing or can they tell you other words to describe this kind of behaviour? Ask the children what they could say to Jonny to make him feel better.

She talks funny

Tell the children about Fiona.

> Fiona used to live in a different part of the country and came to school in the middle of the term. She spoke in a different accent to the other children and some of her words were unusual. Helen, one of the girls in the class, helped Fiona to settle into the class, but some others started teasing her about the way she spoke. This made Fiona upset and she began to dislike school.

Ask the children to think about what people could do to make Fiona feel better about talking in a different way. Ask volunteers to say:

▶ what Helen could do
▶ what the teacher could do
▶ what the other children could do
▶ what Fiona's parents could do.

Write their suggestions on the board or flip-chart. This is what happened…

> Helen kept being Fiona's friend and asked her to teach her some of the unusual words she had used at her last school. The teacher talked to all the children about regional accents and dialects that are usual in different parts of the country. She told them about Gaelic and Welsh and how these are being taught to children so that these languages won't be lost. She asked each child to find out three words that are used in other parts of the UK. The other children began to see Fiona as someone special and not just different.

Fiona's parents were invited to school to talk about the dialect and customs in their part of the UK.

Oki's trousers

In Oki's school in the summer, children were not allowed to do handstands in the playground unless they were wearing trousers. Oki loved to do handstands but trousers were very hot in summer, so she asked her mum to get her some thin trousers. None of the shops had any in the school colour, so Grandma made Oki some out of school dress material.

Oki had three pairs – one very plain, one with lots of pockets and one with a zip. The next day she went to school feeling very good about herself wearing the trousers until some of the boys started teasing her about them and saying she looked like a clown.

Ask the children to think about how this teasing made Oki feel and collect their words.

Ask volunteers to tell you what people could do about this teasing and to finish these sentences…

▸ 'Her friends could…'
▸ 'The teacher could…'
▸ 'She could…'

Oki would feel…

sad
fed up
angry
noticed
different
a bit scared
not liked.

This is what really happened. Oki didn't mind being teased because she could do handstands and that was all that mattered to her. Oki's girl friends wanted to do handstands, thought the trousers were a good idea and wanted some. The headteacher saw Oki in the trousers and said how sensible they were. The other girls asked their mums if they could have some and Oki's grandma was asked if she could make some more or if she would lend people the pattern. In no time at all, all the girls at Oki's school were wearing summer trousers made out of school dress material.

Research related activity

What can you do if you see someone being bullied?
In the bullying research mentioned on page 9 a Year 1 girl drew the picture below about what she could do to help if she saw someone being bullied.

Ask your children to think about what they could do if they saw someone teasing someone else and if it was hurtful teasing. Ask them to draw a picture of someone teasing someone in a bullying way.

Ask them to put themselves in the picture doing something that will help. Show their pictures to the group and talk about what they have drawn and written. Count up how many said they would go for help. How many said they would help? If so, what kinds of things could they safely do?

Did any say they would comfort the person? If so, what did they do? Did any say they would do nothing? If so, why did they say this? Talk about the responsibilities of people who see someone bullying.

Add some of their pictures and writing to your display around the poster. During your work on this theme, use your library to look out for – and encourage children to find – story picture books with characters who tease or who are teased such as:

▸ Rosen, M. (2003) *Snore*, Picture Lions

▸ Stones, R. (1998) *No More Bullying*, Dinosaur Publications

Review

After you have finished this section about teasing, talk with the children about their work and what they have achieved.

Look again at the poster and at the display you have made.

Ask the children which of the teasing pictures on the poster they think are most likely to turn into bullying. Are there any at all?

Ask the children to help you to agree a final speech bubble to add to the display, which will tell other people what they think about teasing.

Share, with other classes or with parents and carers, this poster and the work you have done.

Make sure that everyone in your school knows what they should do if:

▶ somebody bullies by hurtful, unkind teasing
▶ they see or hear someone bullying by hurtful, unkind teasing.

Section 3 – Physically Hurting People's Bodies

In play situations, children are usually happy about touching each other. Some enjoy horse play which can be fun. Sometimes touchings can be hurtful and may be a kind of bullying. In this section we look at situations when 'getting physical' is normal, harmless behaviour and other occasions where repeated hurting is bullying and not fun for the person being hurt.

Physical hurting people's bodies?

Section 3 – Physically Hurting People

Talk with the children about touching other people. Ask them to think about all the ways we touch each other, a pet, our family and friends. Ask them to think about the ways we touch other people in our everyday life and in sport.

Explain that some kinds of touching:

- ▶ are kind and loving
- ▶ are unkind and hurtful
- ▶ can be bullying.

Show the poster to the children, reading out each section and discussing it as below. Display the poster on the wall. Add the children's work as you go through the activities.

Poster related activities

I was first, she pushed in
Talk with the children about this scenario. Someone has pushed in front of someone else and they are complaining.

Ask the children to think about how they feel when someone pushes in front. Can they show by their face how they feel?

Ask volunteers to tell you words to show how they would feel.

She pushed in

angry   mad
fed up   irritated
its unfair   unhappy
cross   annoyed
grumpy.

Make a list of the words and read them out later, asking the children to stand up and show by their faces and body language how each word makes them feel.

Ask the children to think about whether this picture shows bullying or not.

Count up the numbers who say that it is not bullying and ask them to try to explain their reasons.

Explain that pushing in isn't really bullying, but it is unkind and selfish behaviour and that we all have to remember to wait our turn.

Stop kicking

Share this picture with the children and read the speech bubbles.

Ask the children to think what might have happened before one child kicked the other. Ask volunteers to say what they think started it.

Ask volunteers to say how they think the person who is being kicked is feeling. Ask them to say how they think the person doing the kicking is feeling. How many of your children think that this is bullying?

Remind them of the difference between unkind and hurtful behaviour and bullying which takes place over and over again when one person really means to hurt another.

I think you three are bullying that little boy. Stop it or I shall have to go for help.

They keep hitting me

Talk about this scenario: here there are several children and one says that the others keep hitting him.

Ask the children to think of a name for the boy who is being hit and to say how he might be feeling.

Ask them how they think the other children feel. Are they enjoying this?

Ask your children if they think this is bullying and count those who say 'yes'. What could they say to the three children?

Stop pulling my hair

Look at this scenario where someone is pulling a girl's hair. Read the first speech bubble with the children: "Stop pulling my hair!"

Ask the children to stand up if this has ever happened to them. Are the people standing up mainly girls with long hair?

Ask each of those standing to tell the group how it feels when someone pulls their hair.

Read the second speech bubble: "It doesn't hurt."

Pulling hair

it does hurt
it pulls your head back
it feels as if your hair
is coming out
it makes your eyes
water
it jerks your neck.

We say it isn't bullying
unless they keep on
doing it.

Ask if everyone agrees that it doesn't hurt. Ask volunteers to tell you what they would say to the second girl. Read the third speech bubble: "You're always doing it." Ask the group if they think that this is bullying. Remind the children that bullying is when people mean to hurt and when they keep on doing it.

Stop fighting

Find the picture where a girl is telling two boys to stop fighting. Do the children think that will make them stop? What else could the little girl do?

Collect and talk about what they say. Ask the children to close their eyes and think about what happened before the fight started and then ask volunteers to tell you. Ask them to finish the sentence: Before the fight I think…

Ask the children to decide whether this is bullying or not. Ask the children to close their eyes, think about and then draw what could happen next. Show the pictures to the group and ask volunteers to talk about theirs before adding some to your display.

She pushed me into the tree again…

Read the speech bubbles with the children. Tell the children that this happens on the way home every day and that the little boy is scared. Count how many children think this is bullying. Ask them to finish the sentence: 'I think that the little boy should…'

Ask the children to draw what they think happens when the little boy gets home. Ask volunteers to tell the group what they would like to say to the big girl.

She scratched me

Here a boy's arm has been scratched by a little girl who is saying that she is sorry.

Ask the children to think of what happened before this. Ask them to draw a picture of what happened and to write a caption or more about it. Share all the pictures with the group and talk about what could have happened. Do any of the children think it was bullying? If so, why?

The boy's scratch seems to be bleeding, so what should he do? The girl has said she's sorry. What can she do to help to make things better? Ask the children to draw the boy or the girl and what happened next. Talk about little hurts happening by accident and about being careful when playing.

She could take him to the medical room.

Medical Room

She tripped me up

In Circle Time ask the children whether they have ever been tripped up. Go around the circle asking each child to use one sentence, either: 'I have never been tripped up,' or "I was tripped up and…"

Talk about the words and phrases they use and make a list of them. Look again at the poster and ask the children to think whether this is an accident, unkind behaviour or bullying.

Ask the children to make three groups according to which of these they think it is. Ask the children who think it is bullying to give their reasons.

> ## I was tripped up and…
>
> I fell over
> I hurt my hand
> my leg was bleeding
> I tore my dress
> I got all dirty
> my mum was cross
> she didn't mean it
> he said he was sorry.

Further activities

What would you say to Muhjah?

Tell the children this story:

> Muhjah was a big, strong boy aged six who lived quite near to the Infant school. He was always kind and thoughtful and always made sure that he didn't hurt anyone or anything. On the way home two boys from a different class walked his way. They didn't like Muhjah and used to push him about on the way home. Soon Muhjah was afraid to walk to and from school. He was afraid to tell in case the boys hurt him more but he didn't want to fight back. His parents were worried; they didn't know why Muhjah was unhappy.

> ## We would say...
>
> tell your mum
> get help from your teacher
> stay at school later
> ask your mum to meet you
> tell the boys you'll go for help
> hurt them back
> kick them
> run fast.
>
> We think, 'get help from your teacher' is best.

Ask the children to think about whether this is bullying. Ask them to raise one hand if they think 'yes' and to stand up if they think 'no'. Ask volunteers to tell you their reasons for their response. Remind the children that Muhjah is big and strong but doesn't like to hurt people. Ask them to think about what he should do. Ask volunteers to tell the group. Make a list of their responses.

Read the list with the children and ask them to decide which one is the best thing to do. Talk about these options. Encourage the children to tell Muhjah to tell a trusted adult.

Wyn's untidy work

> Wyn could get a friend to go with her to ask the teacher if she could sit at a different table and tell the teacher why.

In the classroom Wyn could not get on with her work because the children on her table were always nudging her and making her spoil her work. It happened every day and she didn't know what to do. The teacher got cross with her, but Wyn was afraid to tell about the other children nudging her in case they hurt her in the playground.

Ask the children if they think this is bullying. Note the number who say 'no'. Ask why they say 'no'.

What could Wyn do? Ask the children to draw what they think. Share all the pictures with the children and ask them to choose the safest thing to do.

Don't keep poking me with your pencil Jill!

Jill and Ann aren't getting on with their work at all. They are messing around and Jill is poking Ann with her pencil.

Ask the children what they think the teacher will say to them. Will the teacher say that Jill is bullying? Ask the children to draw what happens next with the teacher and the two girls. Ask them to give all the people speech bubbles to show what they are saying.

Ask the children to raise a thumb if they think Jill is bullying the other girl. If any do, talk about why they think so.

Stop pushing

Ask the children if any of them have been pushed over in the playground. Count up those who say 'yes' and ask for volunteers to say whether it was an accident or on purpose.

Ask volunteers to say how it makes them feel when someone pushes them. Talk about accidental pushings and how they can be avoided. Ask volunteers to say what someone could do or say if they accidentally pushed someone. Talk about deliberate pushing.

Ask the children to draw a picture of someone pushing someone over in the playground. Ask them to write what they would say to the person if they were sure they had meant to push them over. Collect and talk about what they have written.

Choose some of their pictures and writing to add to the display. Remind the children that someone who often pushes someone on purpose is acting in a bullying way. We should all take care to respect people's body space.

Please don't do that

Tell the children that a little boy called Zac sat next to a little girl who kept poking him with her elbow. She thought it was funny, but Zac got a bit fed up about it. He said, very politely, "Don't do that," but the little girl took no notice. Jacob sat nearby and saw what was happening.

In Circle Time ask the children to finish the sentence: 'I think that Jacob could…' Make a list of all their suggestions.

Read the list to the children and ask them to try to put it in order with the best idea at the top. You could put their suggestions into speech bubbles and add the list to your display.

He keeps strangling me

One day Ben and Caleb were playing in the playground and Ben pulled on Caleb's neck. Caleb said that Ben was strangling him.

We don't think this is bullying. It is dangerous behaviour.

Ask the children if they think that Ben was really strangling Caleb. What is strangling?

Explain that our necks are very weak parts of our body and need to be protected. Explain that if we hurt people's necks it could be very dangerous and perhaps really lead to strangling.

Talk about the danger of pulling the ends of scarves or ties and that they could tighten around someone's neck.

Ask if they think this is bullying. Count how many say 'yes' and ask for their reasons.

Research related activity

How does a bullied person feel?

In the bullying research mentioned on page 9 a Year 1 girl drew this picture about how she thought a bullied person feels.

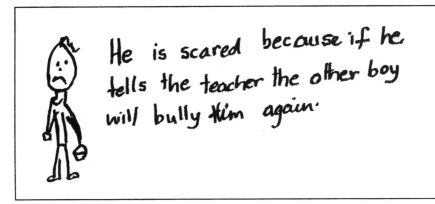

He is scared because if he tells the teacher the other boy will bully him again.

It is important to reassure children who might be afraid of retaliation. Does your behaviour policy make it clear how you help a person who is bullied? Explain to the children what will happen if a child is really bullied in your school. Explain the steps that will be taken if this does occur, how you will deal with it and whether you might involve either or both children's parents. If you use the No Blame Approach this will be easy!

Talk about the feelings of the bullied person – does the bully always realise how the bullied person feels? Explain that sometimes a bully might think it is clever or fun and not quite realise how the bullied person feels.

Ask the children to think about a bully – what they look like, the things they do. Ask them to draw this bully and to write down why they think the bully does it and how it makes the bully feel. Have they fallen into the stereotype trap of drawing the bully as big and strong? Talk about bullies as being ordinary children who have got it wrong about how they play with other children. Explain that anyone can be a bully – it's what they do, not what they look like that makes someone a bully.

We think a bully is...

strong
powerful
horrid
big
tall.

We think a bully means to hurt.
We think a bully might not know how scared the bullied person is.

During your work on this theme, use your library to look out for – and encourage children to find – story picture books with characters who hurt people's bodies or physically bully them. Books such as:

▸ McKee, D. (1987) *Two Monsters*, Random House

▸ Lester, H. (1995) *Me First*, Macmillan

▸ Impey, R. (1993) *The Trouble with the Tucker Twins*, Picture Puffins

---

Review

After you have finished this section about physical bullying talk with the children about their work and what they have achieved.

Look again at the poster and at the display you have made.

Ask the children to decide which of the pictures on the poster are most likely to turn into bullying. Are there any at all?

Ask the children to help you to agree a final speech bubble to add to the display, which will tell other people what they think about physical bullying.

Share, with other classes or with parents this poster and the work you have done.

Make sure that everyone in your school knows what they should do if:

▸ somebody bullies by hurting people's bodies in some way
▸ they see or hear someone physically bullying by hurting people's bodies.

Section 4 – Verbal Bullying

Children talk about each other and in front of each other and may well say things that can be hurtful or laugh in an unkind way. Sometimes these hurts are not intentional but when it is deliberate and directed at the same person over and over again it is a kind of bullying. In this section we examine different scenarios that may or my not be verbal bullying.

Verbal bullying?

Section 4 – Verbal Bullying

Remind the children of the work done in Section 1 about name-calling. Explain that there are other ways of hurting people by saying things that are hurtful and unkind or by laughing in an unkind way. Remind them that it is not only the words we use that can hurt people's feelings, but the way we say them.

Share the poster with the children, reading out each section and discussing it as below. Display the poster on the wall. Add the children's work as you go through the activities.

Poster related activities

She's always arguing with me
Look at what these two children are saying. They have been having a quarrel and one says that the other one keeps arguing.

It can be good if you listen to each other. It can be bullying if one shouts and won't listen.

Ask the children to think what arguing means. Can any of them tell you?

Ask for a show of hands if they have ever argued. Ask volunteers to tell what they have argued about. Ask them if arguing can ever be bullying – collect responses and ask volunteers to explain how it can be bullying. Ask them if arguing can ever be a good thing – collect responses. Ask volunteers to give their reasons.

HOORAY!

We shout...

in the playground
at a football match
when we're cross
on sports day
when we argue
if it's windy
when people don't listen
if we're a long way away
if we know we're right
when we call the dog.

Stop shouting
Ask the children to raise a hand if they ever shout. Ask volunteers to say where and when they shout.

Make a list of what they say. Read the list with your children and ask them when they think it's good to shout and when it is bad to shout. Draw coloured rings around the bad ones.

Ask the children if they think that shouting can ever be bullying and ask volunteers for their reasons.

Ask the children to draw a picture of 'good' or 'bad' shouting and choose some for the display.

60

You're fat aren't you?

Look at this picture with the children and ask them to think if this can ever be a kind thing to say to anyone. Ask them to finish the sentence: 'I think it's a… thing to say.'

Ask them to raise a thumb if they would like someone to say this to them.

Ask them to touch their nose if they would say this to someone else. Talk about making this kind of personal remark to someone. How would the person feel? Ask the children to think when this kind of remark could become bullying and make a note of their responses.

> **If someone called me fat…**
>
> I would be hurt.
> I wouldn't like them.
> They wouldn't be my friend.
> I'd not want to play.
> I'd say that's unkind.
> I would feel bad inside.

Tell the children about the loving mother who might say something like this to her chubby baby – would that be bullying? Why not?

Remind the children that it is the way that things are said that can make words bullying or not bullying.

They keep saying horrid things about me

Here are two girls saying horrid things about another. Ask the children if they have ever had people saying unkind or horrid things about them. Ask them to show you with their face and body how that would have made them feel.

Talk about how the girl would feel if what they said was true. Finish the sentence: 'If it is true she would feel…' Make a list of these feelings words. Talk about how she would feel if what they said was not true.

> **If it's true she would feel…**
>
> sad
> unhappy
> they're mean
> angry
> hurt
> sore inside.

Finish the sentence: 'If it is not true she would feel…' Make a second list with these feelings words. Look at the lists and put rings around words that appear in both lists. Talk about why this could be.

Explain to the children that saying horrid things about someone, especially if it is not true can be a kind of bullying. Display these lists near the poster. Remind them that even if what they say is true, saying unkind things hurts people's feelings and it's better to say kind things. There is always something good to say.

She keeps laughing about me

Remind the children of the lists they made about the girls who were saying horrid things and if you have displayed them, read them with the children.

Ask the children if they think that the girls in this picture are laughing in a kind way at the other. Talk about how you feel if someone's laughing about you – or laughing at you. Ask volunteers to tell you when someone laughing at you can be fun for everyone.

I like people to laugh at me when...

I tell a joke
I do something funny
I am clowning about
I'm trying to cheer them up.

Ask the children to finish the sentence: 'I like people to laugh at me when…' Use 'change places' for repeats and allow children to pass. Ask the children to tell you when laughing can be hurtful and horrid. Ask them to finish this sentence: 'I don't like it if people laugh at me when…'

Collect their responses. Ask the children to draw two pictures on one piece of paper, one where people are laughing kindly at someone and one where people are laughing unkindly. Ask the children to label their pictures or write about the two occasions. Remind them that unkind laughter can be bullying.

C-c-can I play?

First, talk to the children about grown-ups who stutter or stammer. (Stammering is with halting altercation, a stutter is stammer with repeating first consonants of a word.) They may have seen the TV programme *Open All Hours* in which a humorous situation of a stuttering shopkeeper is depicted.

Explain that usually people who have a stutter don't find this funny and are often very embarrassed about it. They find it very difficult to talk at all. This is made worse if people make fun of the way they speak. Read the speech bubbles with the children.

It would help if we...

listened carefully
gave them time to speak
didn't finish their sentences
waited until they finished
didn't mock them
didn't make fun of them.

Ask them to think about what they could do to help someone who stammers, stutters or has any another speech difficulty. Ask them to finish the sentence: "It would help someone who stutters if we…" Remind the children that repeatedly mocking or making fun of the way children speak is a kind of bullying.

He says I'm dim

Look at the picture of these two boys. One is saying that Carl gets work wrong and that he is dim.

We would feel...

sad
upset
angry with ourselves
fed up
annoyed

Ask the children to think how Carl will feel when he hears this. Ask them to finish the sentence: 'I think Carl will feel…' Ask the children how they feel when they get their work wrong. Make a list of their responses.

Ask the children to make their face and body look as if they were feeling like this. Would it make them feel better if someone said they were dim? Ask volunteers to tell you what kinds of things would make them feel better.

Ask the children if they think Carl was being bullied. Count those who say 'yes' and ask them to explain their reasons.

Explain that verbal bullying is when someone says things that they know will hurt you and keeps on saying them even though they know you are feeling hurt.

They're saying rude things about me

Look at this picture of Maysoon saying that people are saying rude things about her. Talk about what 'rude' means (unkind, impolite, bad-mannered, uncouth).

Ask the children how they think Maysoon is feeling. Ask volunteers to finish the sentence, 'I think Maysoon is feeling…' Ask the children how they think the two girls are feeling. Ask volunteers to finish the sentence, 'I think the girls are feeling…'

Don't say things like that. You can see it is hurting Maysoon.

Ask the children to think about whether it matters if the things they are saying are true or not. Ask them to decide which is most hurtful:

▸ saying horrid things that are untrue about someone
▸ saying something horrid that is true about someone.

Ask them to make two groups to show what they think.

Explain to the children that saying unkind, horrid things about someone is hurtful and that it can be bullying if people keep on doing it, whether it is true or not. Ask them to draw themselves and what they would say to the two girls.

Further activities

Poor Jo – she doesn't know anything

Tell the children about Jo, who was six and new to the school.

> On her first day she got lost and ended up in the wrong classroom. On her second day she used the wrong book for her work. On the third day she got all her maths work wrong. On the fourth day the teacher tried hard to help her, but she spilt paint all over someone's best work. In the playground that morning some of the children started chanting about Jo; they made up a song about her not being able to do things and getting things wrong. Jo started to cry and then it was time to go inside.

Ask the children to think whether this was bullying.

Ask them to finish one of these three sentences:

- ▶ 'I think it was bullying because…'
- ▶ 'I think it was not bullying because…'
- ▶ 'I think it could turn into bullying if…'

Count how many say it is bullying. Ask volunteers to say what they could do to help Jo. Ask volunteers to say what they think the teacher could do to help Jo. Ask the children to draw Jo in the playground and draw what they are doing to help her to feel better.

I could get help from the teacher in the playground and then play with Jo to cheer her up.

It's catching

Tell the children that some people have skin that looks spotty or itchy. A skin illness called eczema can make skin look very sore but other people can't catch it. Tell them the story of Hasad.

> Hasad had eczema on his legs and had to have special cream and wear long trousers to protect his skin. Some of the children in his class were very unkind to Hasad when he was doing PE, telling other children that his eczema was catching and that people mustn't touch him or play with him.

> Hasad began to worry about what the children were saying and didn't like doing PE. He kept leaving his shorts at home so that he couldn't do PE and his teacher began to get cross with him. Ask the children to think about who could make Hasad feel better about his eczema and what people could do.

Ask volunteers to finish these sentences:

- ▶ 'The teacher could…'
- ▶ 'Hasad's friends could…'
- ▶ 'The school nurse could…'
- ▶ 'Hasad could…'

Explain to the children that spreading rumours about someone is not only unkind and hurtful, but it can cause unhappiness to a lot of people and, if it is not stopped, can turn into a kind of bullying.

Look at Big-ears

Tell the children this story about Sirap.

He came to school after having a very short haircut and someone said that his ears stuck out. People in the classroom started whispering about Sirap's ears and at last he heard them. When Sirap's best friend said he was still his friend even though his ears stuck out, Sirap shouted at him to 'shut up' and the teacher asked what was going on.

> A good ending would be for the children to say they were sorry and never to talk about his ears again.

Ask the children to finish one of these sentences:

- ▶ 'I think the teacher could…'
- ▶ 'I think his best friend could…'
- ▶ 'If I were Sirap I would…'

Ask the children to think up a good ending to this story.

> The people who started the rumour should be told that they were wrong and that this is bullying.

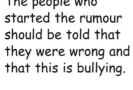

Don't play with her!

Shona had been very ill and when she came back to school she had to have injections and sometimes stay indoors if it was very cold or wet. Three of the girls were very sorry for Shona and helped her in the classroom and played with her in the playground.

Two other girls were very unkind and started saying unkind and untrue things about Shona and telling others not to play with her. Soon only the three friends would play with Shona and she was very upset.

I think the children should be told the truth about Shona's illness.

Shona couldn't sleep at night and didn't want to come to school. Her parents were worried. The teachers were worried.

Talk to the children about saying untrue things or spreading rumours about people. Explain that this really is bullying and that grown-ups need to know that this is happening so that they can do something about it.

Ask volunteers to say what the children, teachers and the school could do about it.

It's not true

Ask the children to think about whether anyone has ever said anything about them, their friends or their family that is not true. Ask volunteers to say how they would feel if someone did this. Collect their words to make a list.

Remind the children about not spreading rumours and ask them to think of a good ending to finish this story.

Sid was angry and fed up because people kept saying his mum didn't love him – just because his mum never came to school to see his work, or came to watch him at sports days. He knew his mum did really love him, but…

angry
unhappy
cross
fed up
miserable
lonely.

Research related activity

Verbal bullying hurts

In the bullying research mentioned on page 9 it was noticed that there was a growing awareness of verbal bullying at Year 2. One quarter of the children who depicted bullying drew someone being verbally bullied. One Year 2 girl drew this picture and wrote about verbal bullying.

To find out what your children think of as bullying ask them to draw a picture of someone who has been bullied. Ask older children to write what is happening in their picture. Ask children who are not yet writing for themselves to tell you what is happening in their picture and write what they say.

When they have all finished their drawing and writing come together as a whole group and talk about what they have said. You may like to make a note of the different ways they have depicted bullying in their pictures. You could devise your own categories or use the six categories from this book.

Talk with the children about the different ways they have drawn bullying. Remind them that what might be a joke to one child is really upsetting to another and that we are all different.

> In the research project one child wrote...
>
> "hitting
> calling names
> saying stuff about thier family etc."

What we say and what we do will affect different people in different ways. It is important to remember this before we say and do things that people might find hurtful.

During your work on this theme, use your library to look out for – and encourage children to find – story picture books with characters who hurt people's feelings by saying hurtful things or who verbally bully them.

Books such as:

▸ Wyllie, S. (1995) *A Flea in the Ear,* Hodder Children's Books

▸ Keller, H. (1982*) Cromwell's Glasses*, Hippo Books

▸ Kasza, K. (1994) *The Rat and the Tiger,* Simon & Schuster.

Review

After you have finished this section about verbal bullying talk with the children about their work and what they have achieved.

Look again at the poster and at the display you have made.

Remind the children which of the pictures on the poster are most likely to turn into bullying. Are there any at all?

Ask the children to help you to agree a final speech bubble to add to the display, which will tell other people what they think about verbal bullying.

Share, with other classes or with parents and carers, this poster and the work you have done.

Make sure that everyone in your school knows what they should do if:

▸ somebody bullies by using words that will hurt people's feelings in some way
▸ they see or hear someone bullying by using words that will hurt people's feelings.

Section 5 – Taking, Breaking and Threatening

Sometimes innocent behaviour under these headings can be misconstrued as bullying, but more often than not this kind of aggressive behaviour is bullying. This section contains examples of bullying and non bullying behaviour under these three headings, and children are helped to decide which is which.

Taking, breaking and threatening?

Section 5 - Taking, Breaking and Threatening

Remind the children of the work done in the other four sections about bullying.

Explain that there are other ways of bullying when children:

▸ take other children's possessions

▸ break children's things

▸ threaten other children.

Did they realise that these could be ways of bullying? Share the poster with the children, reading out each section and discussing it as below. Display the poster on the wall and add the children's work as you go through the activities.

Poster related activities

Give me your lunch biscuit
Ask the children to touch their nose if someone has ever asked them for some of their lunch. Talk about swapping items of lunch from lunch boxes and whether this can be a good or bad thing. Talk about this picture where someone is asking for someone's lunch.

Ask the children whether they think this could be bullying and to finish one of these sentences: 'I think it is bullying because…' or 'I think it is not bullying because…' Remind the children that bullying is deliberate (which this is) and that it is carried on over a period of time: is this?

Ask volunteers to tell you what they would do if someone asked for some of their lunch. Jot down what the children say. Does everyone agree that these are the correct things to do? Is there a better way?

If you don't keep quiet, I'll beat you up
Talk to the children about what this boy is saying. Ask them to:

▸ put one thumb up if they think he is playing
▸ raise a hand if they think he is threatening
▸ put one hand on a shoulder if they think he is bullying.

Count up how many think it is bullying.

We all think this is bullying.

Ask the children for suggestions about what happened before he said this. Ask the children to finish this sentence: 'I think the little boy should…'

Don't tell about the secret

Ask the children to tell you what they think is happening here and to finish the sentence: 'I think…' Make a list of their various responses.

Ask the children to vote on which they think is most likely. Talk about good and bad secrets.

Ask the children to finish one of these sentences:

'It is a good secret when…' or 'It is a bad secret when…' Do the children think this girl is bullying?

> ## We think this might be…
>
> a good secret about a present for mum or a teacher who is leaving. We don't want to spoil the surprise.
> We don't think this is bullying.

You shouldn't pick those flowers

Ask volunteers to tell you what they think is happening here. After everyone who wants to tell has had their turn ask them to vote on whether it is:

▸ someone warning about picking flowers
▸ someone picking flowers for a good reason
▸ someone bullying about telling
▸ someone threatening.

Make sure everyone only has one vote by asking them to stand in a certain place according to their answer. Count up the votes. Discuss with the children the various interpretations of this scenario. Ask older children to work in pairs to role-play what happened before and after. Explore the various interpretations. Talk about not jumping to conclusions and about listening to both sides.

Go and get me some money or…

Ask the children to look at the size of these children. Can there be a good explanation for what the big boy says? Talk about this kind of threatening behaviour and make sure the children realise that it is bullying.

Ask the children to think about how the little boy is feeling. Collect their feelings words and make a list to share. Ask the children to think about what the little boy can do. Ask them to finish the sentence: 'I think the little boy…'

Sorry. I was only playing

Ask the children to close their eyes and think of a time when something went wrong and they said, "I was only playing." Ask volunteers to talk about this.

Now talk about the picture where the little girl says, "You've broken my bag now." Ask the children to think about what might have happened. Ask them to finish the sentence: 'I think what happened was...'

Talk about all the responses the children give. Ask the children whether they think the girl with the bag was being bullied.

Don't tell Mrs Jones

Ask the children to think of times when they have broken something. Ask them to tell you how they felt.

Talk about the picture and the little boy saying he will tell Mrs Jones. Ask the children what they would say to the little boy about owning up. Ask the children to put a thumb up if they think this is bullying.

Ask them to put a thumb down if they do not think it is bullying. Count how many say it is bullying and ask volunteers to say why they think this.

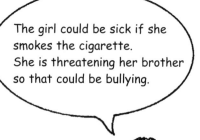

We felt...

sad
unhappy
cross
worried
scared to tell
ashamed
silly.

Do you want a fag?

Examine this scenario with the children.

Explain that the boy is trying to persuade the girl to do something she knows is wrong and the little boy is going to tell. The girl then says that she will 'bash up' her little brother.

The girl could be sick if she smokes the cigarette.
She is threatening her brother so that could be bullying.

Ask the children to think what could be bullying in this picture. Is it:

▸ the boy giving the girl a cigarette
▸ the little boy saying he will tell
▸ the girl saying she will bash up her brother?

Talk with the children about what the little boy should do. Ask volunteers to say what could happen.

Further activities

It's mine
Tell the children this story:

> Kathy had been given some new special pens for her birthday and she took them to school. She put them on the table where her group were doing their writing and drawing. Jay picked up the blue one and started to use it and Kathy was angry. "It's mine!" she said, "You're stealing." Jay gave it back and said he thought that she had put them there for everyone to use. Azif said that he thought that taking things was a kind of bullying and that made everyone stop and stare at Jay.

Ask the children if they think this is stealing, bullying or whether it is something else. Ask them to finish one of these sentences:

'I think it is…' or 'I think it is not…'

Ask the children to think of the children's feelings. How do they think Kathy felt? How do they think Jay felt? Ask volunteers to say what they would have said if they had been in that group doing their work. Ask the children to draw a good ending to this story.

Jay said he was sorry and then Kathy said that everyone could share the pens

Prove it!
Tell the children this story:

> One day when Simon was walking home from school he met up with some children from another school. They told Simon that they were a gang and he could join if he wanted to but he would have to prove he was brave. They said he would have to go to the sweet shop and steal some sweets. Simon was worried about this because he knew that stealing was wrong but he really did want to join the gang.

Talk about this story with the children. What would they say to Simon? What would they say to the gang? Is this threatening? Is this bullying? Collect responses from the children and see if they can come to a group decision.

Hayley doesn't want to go to school

Tell the children this story:

Hayley is six years old and is not happy about going to school. In the playground, some of the children keep taking her things and throwing them about. Her mum was cross when she went home with her woolly hat dirty and torn. Hayley didn't know what to do to stop this, so she pretended that she was ill and couldn't go to school.

I'm glad I told my teacher. It's OK now.

Ask the children if they have ever felt like Hayley – not wanting to go to school because of feeling unhappy there.

Ask them to touch their ear if they have felt like this. Can volunteers tell you why they felt like that?

Ask the children to think about what Hayley could do. Collect their responses and go through them one by one. Is there one really good thing that she could do?

Ask the children to draw Hayley on a good day when things are better. Ask them to write a caption or speech bubble.

Taking things home

Zara's mother wondered why she never took any of her paintings and models home to show the family. On the school's open day the teacher told her mother that Zara never wanted to take her things home and showed her some of the lovely things she had made.

That night Zara and her mother talked about this and Zara told her about some children who took and spoiled her work on the way home. Ask the children why they think the children spoiled Zara's work. Talk about this kind of bullying and how Zara felt.

The bullies:

were jealous
wanted to show off
wanted to act big
didn't think it was bullying
didn't think about Zara's feelings.

Ask older children to work in pairs with one being Zara and one her mother. Ask them to role-play the scene where Zara tells her mother about the bullying. Can they show their feelings in their face and body language? Can they think of the right things to say? Ask volunteers to say what Zara and her mum could do. Will some pairs show their role-play to the whole group?

Owning up

Talk with the children about what to do when they break or spoil things at school. Tell the children about something precious that you yourself broke and what you did about it. Tell them how you felt.

When I broke my mum's best ornament I felt very angry with myself. My mum was angry at first. Then she forgave me.

Ask volunteers to tell you about something they broke at school or at home and what they did about it. How did they feel? Did they always own up? Did they sometimes pretend that they had not broken it?

Ask the children to finish the sentence: 'When I broke something, I...'

Ask the children to role-play this in pairs – one to pretend that they broke something and the other to be the grown-up.

Ask them to think of what they would both say and do. They should change places so that they have a turn at being the grown-up.

Ask volunteers to show you their role-play. Did some of the grown-ups get angry? Did some of the children pretend they hadn't broken it? Ask the children to think of a slogan about what to do when you break something by accident.

COME ON HARRY

I'll get you on the way home

Vijay hears a boy he doesn't know saying to his friend Harry, "I'll get you on the way home."

Ask the children what they think is happening here.

Could he be helping to take Harry home?

Could he be bullying Harry?

Ask the children to finish the sentence:

'I think the boy is...'

Ask the children to draw a picture of Harry and the boy and to write in it what Harry says.

I'll take that

One day in the playground May sees a girl from another class snatching a book from her friend Lally. The girl shouts, "I'll take that!" and runs off with the book.

Ask the children whether they think these girls are playing or whether they think it is bullying.

Ask for a show of hands and note the number that say it is bullying. Ask these children to explain their reasons for saying it is bullying.

Ask them all to think how this story could end and to draw and write about what happened next.

A happy ending

Lally had her library book in the playground and the library helper was taking it back to the library.

What can you do?

Talk with the children about bullies who deliberately take and break and spoil things.

Ask them to touch their nose if they have ever seen someone doing this and ask volunteers to tell you about what happened, how it made them feel and what they did.

Explain that it can be dangerous to try to stop people doing this, especially if they are bigger children than they are, but there is something they can do.

Ask them to think about this and to finish the sentence:

I could get help from mum or the teacher or someone I trust.

'If I saw someone bullying by taking or breaking things or threatening, I would…'

Ask them what they would say if people said they were 'telling tales'. Should they think about getting help rather than 'telling tales'? Ask them to finish the sentence: 'I would say…'

Research related activity

What can the school do to help?

In the bullying research mentioned on page 9, the picture below is what a Year 1 girl wrote about what the school could do if there was bullying there.

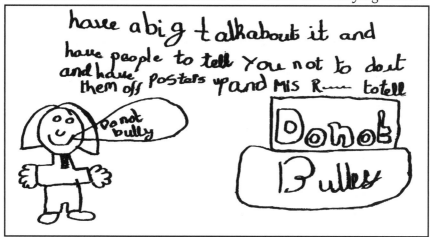

Ask the children to think about what your school already does about bullying. Talk about what happens in your school and how you stop bullying. (If you have a bullying or behaviour policy you could show this to the children.) Ask the children to think about anything else that your school could do.

Ask them to finish this sentence: "I think our school could…" Allow children to 'pass'. Collect their ideas onto a flip-chart and, when all the children have had the chance to say what they think, read through the children's views. Ask them to vote on which ideas they think are the best. Talk about the practicalities of such a policy – is it fantasy or would it work?

If you have a school council, perhaps your children could take any relevant suggestions there. If not, perhaps a group could be chosen to take their suggestions to the headteacher. During your work on this theme, use your library to look out for – and encourage children to find – story picture books with characters who take or break other people's things or who threaten them. Books such as:

▶ Lloyd, D. (1986) *The Stopwatch*, Walker Books

▶ Selway, M. (1994) *I Hate Roland Roberts*, Red Fox

▶ Prater, J. (2001) *I'm Coming to Get You*, Random House

▶ Weigelt, U. (2001) *It Wasn't Me*, North-South Books.

Review

After you have finished this section about bullying concerned with taking, breaking or threatening behaviour talk with the children about their work and what they have achieved.

Look again at the poster and at the display you have made.

Remind the children which of the pictures on the poster are most likely to turn into bullying. Are there any at all?

Ask the children to help you to agree a final speech bubble to add to the display, which will tell other people what they think about these kinds of bullying.

Share, with other classes or with parents and carers, this poster and the work you have done.

Make sure that everyone in your school knows what they should do if:

▸ somebody bullies by taking or breaking their property or by threatening them
▸ they see or hear someone bullying by taking or breaking other children's property or by threatening them.

Section 6 – Excluding

Children are often possessive of their friends and group friendships and may not realise that keeping others out of their group is bullying when it is persistant and deliberate. In this section we look at times when it is okay for children who want to play their games with special friends or teams without intruption, and other times when a deliberate attempt to keep certain children out of groups is bullying.

Session 6 – Excluding

Remind the children of the work done in the other five sections about bullying.

Explain that another way of bullying can be by not letting others join in and by keeping people out of groups. Did they realise this?

Share the poster with the children, reading out each section and discussing it as below. Display the poster on the wall. Add children's work as you go through the activities.

Poster related activities

No you can't play with us

Show the poster to the children and ask them to tell you what is happening. Ask the children whether they think this is bullying. Explain that it is OK to play with your friends and that there will be times when you don't want someone else to join in.

I would say, "This is a game for two people. You can play next."

Ask the children to think of the way these two boys told the third that he couldn't play. Can any of them think of a better way of saying it? Ask the children to finish this sentence: 'I would say…'

Tell them that if children never let someone join in their games or gangs, or always keep one person out that it can turn into bullying.

Go away, we don't want you

Here, two girls are being unkind to Joanne. Ask the children if they think the two girls are bullying the other.

I think Joanne would feel hurt and unwanted.

Collect responses by a show of hands and ask volunteers to justify their responses. Suppose this happened every day and Joanne was never allowed to join in. How would Joanne feel? Ask the children to finish the sentence: 'I think Joanne would feel…'

Ask the children to think whom Joanne could go to for help. Ask volunteers to finish the sentence: 'I think Joanne could…' Could Joanne's friends help? Could the teacher help? What could they do? Talk about the children's responses to these questions.

Please Miss, they won't let me join in
Here, two children are playing catch and won't let Tom join in. He is telling the teacher. In Circle Time, ask the children to think what the teacher could do and to finish the sentence: 'The teacher could…'

Allow children to 'pass' and ask children who repeat someone else's sentence to change places with each other. Jot down what they say and when everyone has had a turn, talk about their responses.

Ask the children to touch their nose if they think this is bullying. Ask them to lift their shoulders if they think it is not bullying.

Explain that it is not bullying if children want to play with their friends, but that it could be bullying if a group of children always keep one child out of their game on purpose and if they mean to leave the child out. Tell them that this is called 'excluding' someone.

She was my friend first
Do the children think that the two girls in this picture are excluding the other girl? Ask them to raise their shoulders if they think this is bullying. Ask those who think it is not bullying to give their reasons.

Talk to the children about their friends. Ask them if they think we own our friends and if we have a right to keep a friend to ourselves. Ask volunteers to say what they think and talk with the group about what each child says. Explain that friends are not like toys or clothes – they don't belong to people.

Talk about sharing friends and having a network of friends who also belong to other networks of friends. Explain that if we share friends we soon have lots of friends, but if we try to keep one friend to ourselves, they may go away and we'll have none. Explain that 'having friends' isn't the same as 'being friendly'. You can be friendly to everyone and have just one or a few real friends.

Ask the children to draw a picture with all their friends in it – friends from school, friends from home and friends in their families. Ask them to write their friends' names. Ask the children to draw another picture, this time of themselves being friendly to someone.

> ## The teacher could…
> ask the two if Tom could join in
> help Tom to find someone else to play with
> find a job for Tom to do
> talk to Tom about children playing games in twos.

We've got a secret

Ask the children to think about what a secret is. Ask them to finish the sentence: 'I think a secret is…' Allow children to 'pass'.

Jot down what they say and when everyone has had a turn, talk about what they said. Talk about good secrets and bad secrets – good ones being lovely surprises and bad ones usually awful things that someone could be afraid about.

Look at what these girls on the poster are saying. Ask the children to think about whether the two girls are being friendly, unfriendly or bullying. Ask them to:

- raise a thumb if they think the children are being friendly
- fold their arms if they think the children are being unfriendly
- kneel up if they think the children are bullying.

Count up the numbers and make a note of them. Ask volunteers to give reasons for their decision.

> **We think…**
>
> 0 of us think the girls are being friendly.
> 12 of us think the children are being unfriendly.
> 11 say they are just unkind.
> 2 of us think it is a kind of bullying.

Explain that even if this isn't bullying this kind of behaviour is nasty and that the two girls are being very unkind in taunting the other.

Don't let him in our team

Ask the children to think whether these three children are bullying the new boy. Ask them to raise an elbow if they think not. Ask these children to make a line and count themselves. Ask volunteers to explain their choice.

Remind the children that not allowing people to join in can be bullying. Explain that everyone has the right to belong – in school or in other outside school groups. Remind them that hurting someone by deliberately keeping them out of a group is bullying. What do they think the new boy should do or say?

> **This is what we think…**
>
> 0 of us think it's kind.
> 6 of us think it's unkind.
> 22 of us think it is bullying.
>
> We all think that the new boy should tell.

Don't talk to her

Ask the children to tell you what they think about this scenario. What could it be about? Ask volunteers to tell you what they think happened before and what is going on.

Jot down their responses and when all the children have had time to respond, talk about what they have said. Could this be bullying? Ask children to raise a hand if they think so. Talk about the phrase 'sending to Coventry'.

Remind them that deliberately excluding someone or not talking to someone is unfriendly, might be bullying and is not the sort of behaviour expected in a friendly school.

Ask them to draw what happened next and to label or write about their drawing.

> ## What happened next?
>
> The girl got help from the teacher, who talked about what happened to everyone in the classroom.
> Then the two girls were very sorry. They didn't mean to bully. They made friends with the other one.
>
>

You're spoiling our game...

Ask the children to think of this scenario: three children are playing a game and another wants to join in. Ask the children to raise a thumb if this has ever happened to them?

Count how many.

Ask volunteers to say why the three children might not want another to join the game and make a note of their responses on a flip-chart or chalk board. Read through their list and ask the children if these are all good reasons or are some unkind reasons? Draw a circle around the good reasons.

Talk about the unkind reasons and how this might make the other child feel.

Ask volunteers to say what could make this into a bullying scenario.

Ask children to draw a happy ending to this scenario.

Further activities

You can't come to my party

Tell the children about Anoop who was not a popular boy in the class. He had three friends in his group and they all worked at the same table. They all got on well together.

One day Ross, a boy in the class, was talking about his birthday party. He said that his mum said he could invite all the boys in the class, but he said he wasn't going to ask Anoop to come. He said he would invite everybody else but not Anoop.

> Everyone except Anoop can come.

Ask the children what they think about that. Ask volunteers to tell the group what they think. Ask the children to think about what Anoop and his three friends could do or say. Ask them to finish one of these sentences:
'I think Anoop could...' or 'I think Anoop's friends could...'

Remind the children that leaving one person out of a group is excluding and is a kind of bullying and ask them to say whether Ross realises he is bullying Anoop in the story.

Mum goes shopping

Remind the children about excluding people from games and play. Tell them this story:

> Mum was going shopping to buy a birthday present for Kate, but she didn't want Kate to go with her because she would see the present. Mum told Kate that she was going shopping with her little brother and sister but that Kate would have to go and stay with her Grandma for the afternoon. Kate wanted to go shopping and she began to cry. Then she said that mum was excluding her and that was bullying.

> I think mum could say she was going for the present and then Kate would understand.

Is Kate right? Is this a kind of bullying? Ask children the reasons for their answers. Ask the children to think about what mum could say to Kate. Collect contributions from the children. Ask them what they would say to Kate and make a list of what they say.

Who's going to the pantomime?

Jack and Kitty were going to the pantomime with their mum and dad. It was one of their Christmas presents. The day before, a cousin had to come to stay with them because her mum was going into hospital. Mum and dad only had four tickets and now there were five of them.

Kitty said that they must not exclude their cousin because that was a kind of bullying, but Dad said…

Ask the children to think about what Dad might say. Ask them to finish the sentence: 'Dad said…'

Ask the children to draw and write a good ending for this story.

Dad said he would stay at home so that mum and the children could go. He said he would give them money for ice creams.

The school outing

Jazzer was excited because the next day his class were going to the seaside to find out about sea life. They had to wear welly boots and take a plastic bag with their lunch and another one to put anything interesting that they might find.

That afternoon after school, Jazzer was playing football with his friends and fell badly and had to go to hospital. Jazzer had sprained his ankle and had to have it bandaged and keep it up on a chair for two days. He could not go on the outing.

Ask the children how they think Jazzer was feeling and to finish the sentence: 'I think Jazzer would feel…'

Collect their responses. Ask the children if this is exclusion. Did any say 'yes'?

Ask the children to think about what Jazzer's class could do to make him feel better about missing the outing.

Ask them to draw a picture and write about what the class could do to make Jazzer feel better about missing the outing.

All the chidren made 'Get Well' cards for Jazzer. Some of them said they missed Jazzer on the outing. Some drew pictures about what they did on the outing and they put these pictures in a big envelope to send to him.

I can't join in

Ask the children whether they've ever felt that they couldn't join in, for example, a game, some work or a team.

Ask volunteers to say what happened and how it made them feel.

Talk about children with special needs who might feel like this.

Ask the children to tell you why children might not be able to join in and make a list of their responses.

Ask children to think about times when children have to be chosen for a special part in a concert or assembly. How do these chosen children feel? Make a list of their responses.

How do those not chosen feel? Make another list.

How can grown-ups try to make sure they are fair when they have to choose someone for something special?

Is not choosing you a kind of bullying?

Children can't join in if they...

are sick
are in a wheelchair
have a broken leg
are in hospital
are going to move away
are going on holiday
are afraid
can't swim or play a game.

Research related activity

Different kinds of bullying

In the bullying research mentioned on page 9 one Year 1 girl drew this picture and wrote about various kinds of bullying.

Talk to the children about all the different kinds of bullying they now know. Ask them to draw a picture of someone being bullied. Can they draw lots of different ways? Share their pictures and make a list of all the different ways the children have depicted bullying.

Are these all pictures of bullying or are some of them of unkind and unpleasant behaviour? Put out two pieces of A1 paper or card – one for bullying and one for not bullying. Ask the children to help you to decide in which set each drawing should go. Make two collages using as many of the cut out pictures as possible. Ask the children to help you to make large speech bubbles about their drawings, naming or labelling the kinds of bullying and the kinds of non-bullying drawings.

Help the children to draw around one child with thick felt pens, to cut it out and to 'dress' the child by using a variety of media – paint, crayon, fabric pieces and coloured paper. Ask children to suggest and help you to make large speech bubbles to say what this child would do if she or he were bullied and add these speech bubbles to the picture. Display the two collages with this picture between them.

During your work on this theme, use your library to look out for – and encourage children to find – story picture-books with characters who won't let people play, who keep them out of their group or who stop them from joining in.

Tell traditional tales such as:

▶ Cinderella – whose ugly sisters won't let her go to the ball – various versions

▶ *The Ugly Duckling*, retold by Kevin Crossley-Holland, Orion.

Review

After you have finished this final section about people who bully by excluding children, talk with them about their work and what they have achieved.

Look again at the poster and at the display you have made.

Remind the children which of the pictures on the poster are most likely to turn into bullying. How many are there? Are there any at all?

Ask the children to help you to agree a final speech bubble to add to the display, which will tell other people what they think about bullying by excluding people.

Share, with other classes or with parents and carers, this poster and the work you have done.

Make sure that everyone in your school knows what they should do if:

▶ somebody bullies by not letting people join in or excluding them from a group
▶ they see or hear someone bullying by not letting people join in or excluding them from a group.

Summary

At the end of these activities your children should have a clear idea of what bullying is and what it isn't.

Perhaps you have coined your own phrase for non-bullying but hurtful behaviour. If so, make sure that everyone in the school uses it. Make sure that this includes all children and adults, including, mid-day supervisors, classroom assistants and parent helpers – who may be on duty in the playground.

You may refer to such non-bullying behaviour as:

▶ hurtful behaviour
▶ unkind behaviour
▶ anti-social behaviour
▶ unfriendly behaviour.

Whatever you call it, make sure that the children know that it is not bullying, but that it is the kind of behaviour that hurts other children and that they have a responsibility to think of how other children feel.

You may like to include this philosophy of unkind but non-bullying behaviour in your behaviour policy and your home/school brochure so that parents and carers will know your definition of bullying and what you do about bullying and unkind behaviour in your school.

Checklist Part 1

You can use these two pages of checklists to elicit the children's views on whether they think they are bullied or not.

Use Part 1 for younger children and both parts for older children. You can add appropriate categories of your own.

You could:

▸ go through the list, a few at a time, during Circle Time
▸ read it to young children, individually or in a small group
▸ give it, or part of it, to older children to complete on their own.

The results will provide you with discussion points for several sessions.

	This week, did anyone:	Tick here	Was it bullying?
1	Call you a fun name		
2	Call you a hurtful name		
3	Tease you in fun		
4	Tease you hurtfully		
5	Say they were only teasing		
6	Make a good joke with you		
7	Help you with your work		
8	Shout at you		
9	Make fun of you		
10	Play a good game with you		
11	Try to trip you up		
12	Make sure you were okay		
13	Say they would hurt you		
14	Share something with you		
15	Try to take something from you		
16	Be a good friend		

Checklist Part 2

	This week, did anyone:	Tick here	Was it bullying?
17	Tease you about your family		
18	Care for you		
19	Try to kick you		
20	Talk about your work with you		
21	Try to hit you		
22	Play outside with you		
23	Try to make you hurt someone		
24	Keep you safe from someone		
25	Try to make you do something you didn't want to		
26	Help you to clear up		
27	Be unkind about how you look		
28	Say you look good		
29	Try to frighten you		
30	Talk about problems with you		
31	Get a gang to pick on you		
32	Play well in a group with you		

Story picture-books

When reading stories to your children look out for all kinds of unkind, thoughtless behaviour or bullying. Finish the story and then go back and talk about the feelings of people who are teased, bullied, persuaded or discriminated against. Talk about the feelings of the teaser or bully. Then talk about what changed so that the story had a happy ending.

Emphasise that the stereotyping of bullies as big, bad and bold, and victims as small, weak and shy, is often untrue. Remind the children that anyone can be a bully, just as anyone can be bullied.

Many interesting and useful storybooks can be found in school and public libraries. Ask the children to look out for books where people are hurt, have their feelings hurt, or are bullied. These stories will provide useful discussions for the whole class.

The following is a list of story picture-books found in most schools. The stories are fun and interesting in their own right, but you can use them to discuss the implications of the actions of the characters and whether some hurtful behaviour could be thought of as bullying.

Wyllie, S. (1995) *A Flea in the Ear*, Hodder Children's Books.
    A book about persuasion. Wily fox persuades the spotted farm dog to go to the pond to get rid of his fleas. But the dog gets even with Fox and saves the chickens.

Fries, C. (2001) *A Pig Is Moving In*, Siphano Picture Books
    This lovely picture-book tries to encourage children not to pre-judge someone.

Burningham, J. (1993) *Aldo*, Red Fox
    Aldo is a lonely child who lives with volatile adults and is sometimes bullied. She is comforted by her imaginary friend.

Walton, R. (2002) *Bertie was a Watchdog*, Walker Books
    Bertie was a very small dog, but he stood up to the big, bad robber and turns out to be a hero.

Cottringer, A. & Whatmore, C. (ill.) (2001) *Buster's Bark*, Orchard Books
    Buster is a small dog with a big bark, until he meets Butch. A story with bright bold illustrations about bullying and friendship.

Greene, C. & Mortimer, A. (ill.) (1999) *Cat and Bear*, Frances Lincoln Ltd.
Cat doesn't like Bear, who bullies and tries to get rid of him.

Keller, H. (1982) *Cromwell's Glasses*, Hippo
Cromwell is a rabbit with a difference – he can't see properly. His family call him names and laugh at him when he tries to help and things go wrong. Eventually he gets glasses and finds he can see. Unfortunately someone makes fun of him before his sister intervenes.

Selway, M. (1995) *I hate Roland Roberts*, Red Fox
Rosie doesn't like sitting next to Roland, who calls her Crybaby, and Gringe,and was with boys who ran off with her Teddy and threw him into a tree. However, she begins to like him and the story ends with her saying 'I like Roland Roberts a lot!'

Prater, J. (2001) *I'm Coming to Get You*, Random House
Tommy thinks that the monster is fierce and frightening until he conquers his fears and controls the situation.

Weigelt, U. (2001) *It Wasn't Me*, North-South books
Everyone blames Raven for stealing Ferret's raspberries but are they right to blame her without proof? A book about prejudice and unfounded allegations.

Briggs, R. (1973) *Jim and the Beanstalk*, Hamish Hamilton
In this story, the giant turns out to be quite different from our expectations.

French, V. (1995) *Lazy Jack*, Walker Books
Poor Jack gets everything wrong – but in the end he is Clever Jack!

Lester, H. (1995*) Me First*, Macmillan Children's Books
Pinkerton Pig pushes in and always wants to be first – until he meets the Sandwich.

Blackman, M. & McCafferty, J. (ill) (1995) *Mrs Spoon's Family*, Andersen Press
Mrs Spoon has a dog and suffers jibes and mockery when she takes in a cat.

Glitz, A. & Swoboda, A. (2001) *Prince Charming and Baabarella (Cat's Whiskers)*, Franklin Walls
The Prince is short-sighted and should wear glasses – a lovely tale for some-one who feels 'different' because of wearing glasses.

Jenkin-Pearse, S. (1992) *Rosie and the Pavement Bears*, Red Fox
Rosie is the smallest in the class and it is not easy putting up with bullies like Ben and Bill. But bullies beware! The pavement bears are here. Rosie finds out that even little people can stand up for themselves.

Graham, B. (1994) *Rose meets Mr Wintergarten*, Walker Books
This book is about rumours. Children say that Mr Wintergarten is mean and horrible, but Rosie goes to ask for her ball back and finds out the truth.

Godden, R. (1975) *The Diddakoi*, Puffin Books
A story of prejudice – bullying – with a happy ending.

Kasza, K. (1994) *The Rat and the Tiger*, Simon & Schuster
Verbal bullying in a good fun story.

Lloyd, D. (1986) *The Stopwatch*, Walker Books
Tom times everything until someone takes his stopwatch. It wasn't really taken – only borrowed.

Impey, R. (1993) *The Trouble with the Tucker Twins*, Picture Puffins
The Tucker twins make Mick's life a misery. How can he stand up for himself when it's two against one? But are the bullies as tough as they make out? Humorous.

The Ugly Duckling, retold by Kevin Crossley-Holland, Orion
The traditional tale of discrimination, exclusion and bullying, until the duckling turns out to be a swan.

Naidoo, B. (1994) *Trouble for Letang and Julie*, Longman
Julie is called rude names at school after letting the pet hamster escape. The teacher discusses teasing and name-calling.

McKee, D. (1987) *Two Monsters*, Random House
Two monsters fall out over their differences of opinion and start a fight that soon gets out of hand.

Books specifically about bullying

Johnson, J. (1998) *Bullies and Gangs,* Watts
Tackles different forms of bullying – sensible advice with opportunities for discussion.

Amos, J. (2001) *Good & Bad: Bully*, Cherrytree
Three stories to provide useful starting points for discussion.

Green, J. & Gordon, M.(1999) *I feel bullied*, Hodder Wayland
Pre-school/infant level – useful as a tool for teachers to discuss bullying behaviour.

Stones, R.(1998) *No More Bullying*, Dinosaur Publications
A little girl tells the story of how she was bullied and what the school did about it.

Powell, J. (1998) *What do we think about bullying?*, Hodder Wayland
This book explores feelings of the bully as well as the bullied child.

A storybook about cancer and bullying

Schulz, C. M. (1991) *Why, Charlie Brown, Why?*, Ravette Books
A story about what happens when Janice gets leukaemia and is called names at school when the treatment makes her hair fall out. Linus goes to her aid and tells the bully why. It all ends happily when the treatment is over and Janice returns to school.

A video and activities about name-calling

Brown, T. (1998) *Broken Toy,* Lucky Duck Publishing Ltd.
Raymond's life is made miserable by bullying. A friend offers some support but when he leaves school, Raymond's misery continues. An accident provides a focus for all those involved to consider the effects of bullying on the victim. This video is for ages 9 to 12 and is suitable only for the older members of your group.

Resources

Robinson, G. & Maines, B.(rev 2000) *Crying for Help*, the No Blame Approach to Bullying, Lucky Duck Publishing Ltd.

Tompkins, C., Wetton, N. & Collins, M., (2003) *Challenging Bullying Behaviour*, Investors in Health, Furnace Drive, Furnace Green, Crawley, West Sussex RH10 6JB. Changing perceptions of school children in Years R-7 of being bullied and how we can challenge bullying behaviour.

Wetton, N. & Collins, M. (2001) *Bullying Matters*, Healthwise, 101 Woodside Business Park, Shore Road, Birkenhead CH41 1EP. Tel: 0151 649 3400.

Useful websites

www.dfee.gov.uk/bullying

www.dontsufferinsilence.com

www.bullying.co.uk – information and advice about bullying for teachers, children and parents

www.antibullying.net – information and advice about bullying

www.childline.org.uk – confidential helpline for children.

www.wiredforhealth.gov.uk – provides information for delivery of health education in schools

www.dfes.gov.uk/a-z/CITIZENSHIP.html

www.rospa.com

Other Resources

Collins, M. (1995) *Keeping Safe – safety education for young children*, Forbes Publications Ltd.

Collins, M. (1997) *Keep Yourself Safe – an activity based resource for primary schools*, Lucky Duck Publishing Ltd. (OUT OF PRINT)

Collins, M. (1998) *Let's Get it Right for Nursery Children*, Forbes Publications Ltd.,

Collins, M. (2001) *Circle Time for the Very Young*, Lucky Duck Publishing Ltd.

Collins, M. (2001) *Because We're Worth It.*, Lucky Duck Publishing Ltd.

Collins, M. (2002) *Circling Round Citizenship*, Lucky Duck Publishing Ltd.

Collins, M. (2002) *Because I'm Special*, Lucky Duck Publishing Ltd.

Collins, M. (2003) *Enhancing Circle Time for the Very Young*, Lucky Duck Publishing Ltd.

Collins, M. (2004) *Circling Safely*, Lucky Duck Publishing Ltd.

DfEE (2001) Promoting Children's Mental Health within Early Years and School Settings.

Milicic, Neva (1994) *It's Good to be Different – Stories from the Circle*, Lucky Duck Publishing Ltd. (OUT OF PRINT)

Robinson, G. & Maines, B. (1995) *Celebrations*, Lucky Duck Publishing Ltd.

Wetton, N. & Collins, M. (1998) *Ourselves Resource Pack* (Watch), BBC Educational Publishing.

Wetton, N. & Collins, M. (2003) *Pictures of Health,* Belair Publications Ltd.

White, M. (1999) *Picture This – Guided Imagery* (CD and booklet), Lucky Duck Publishing Ltd.

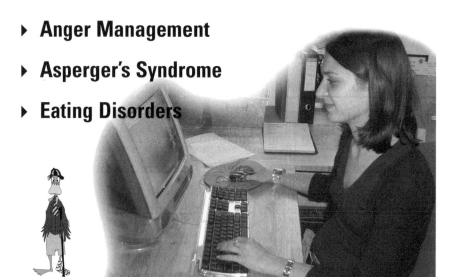